**MY**

Name
_____
Address
_____

Passport Number
_____
Country of issue
_____
Blood Type
_____

_____

Contact Number
_____
Email Address
_____

_____

EMERGENCY CONTACTS

Name
_____
Relationship
_____
Address
_____

Contact Number
_____
Email Address
_____

INSURANCE DETAILS

Provider
_____
Policy Number
_____
Claim number
_____

_____

BASICS	HEALTH
☐ Passports	☐ Motion Sickness Tablets
☐ Visa	☐ Anxiety Tablets
☐ Travel Docs	☐ Inhaler
☐ Accommodation Docs	☐ Vitamins
☐ Travel Insurance	☐ Birth Control
☐ Medical Insurance	☐ Insect Repellant
☐ Drivers License	☐ Pain Relief
☐ Cash	☐ First-Aid Kit
☐ Credit Cards	☐ Cotton Balls
☐ Debit Card	Other

BASICS	VACCINATIONS
☐ Itinerary	
☐ Maps & Directions	☐ Tetanus
☐ Travel Guides	☐ Typhoid
☐ Travel locks & Keys	☐ Typhus
☐ Itinerary	☐ Polio
☐ Emergency Money	☐ Cholera
☐ Documentation photocopies	☐ Hepatitis
☐ Jewelry	☐ Malaria
☐ Other	☐ Other

CLOTHES	QTY	OUTWEAR	QTY
☐ Underwear		☐ Jackets	
☐ Socks		☐ Coats	
☐ Bras		☐ Raincoat	
☐ Vests		☐ Gloves	
☐ Sleepwear		**FOOTWEAR**	
☐ Robe		☐ Sandals/Flipflops	
☐ Skirts		☐ Dress Shoes	
☐ Dresses		☐ Slippers	
☐ Shirts		☐ Leisure Shoes	
☐ Tops		**HYGIENE**	
☐ Trousers		☐ Toothbrush	
☐ Shorts		☐ Toothpaste	
☐ Jeans		☐ Mouthwash	
☐ Swimsuits		☐ Dental Floss	
☐ Beachwear		☐ Washcloth	
☐ Exercise Clothes		☐ Soap/Shower Gel	
☐ Suits		☐ Shampoo	
☐		☐ Conditioner	
☐		☐ Comb	

	QTY	ELECTRONICS
☐ Brush		☐ Cell Phone
☐ Styling Products		☐ Charger
☐ Curling / Flat Iron		☐ Tablet
☐ Sunscreen		☐ Camera
☐ Moisturizer		☐ Ipod / MP3 Player
☐ Lip Balm		☐ Batteries
☐ Contact Lens		☐
☐ Saline Solutions		☐
☐ Sun glasses		☐
☐ Reading Glasses		☐
☐ Hand Sanitizer		☐
☐ Deodorant		☐
☐ Perfume		☐
☐ Hair brush		☐
☐ Make-up		☐
ACCESSORIES		☐
☐ Scarves / Ties		☐
☐ Belts		☐
☐ Watches		☐

OTHER ITEMS TO PACK

☐	☐
☐	☐
☐	☐
☐	☐
☐	☐
☐	☐
☐	☐
☐	☐
☐	☐
☐	☐
☐	☐
☐	☐
☐	☐
☐	☐
☐	☐
☐	☐
☐	☐
☐	☐
☐	☐

DATE/DAY	
PLACE I VISITED	
PEOPLE I MET	

DATE/DAY	
PLACE I VISITED	
PEOPLE I MET	

DATE/DAY	
PLACE I VISITED	
PEOPLE I MET	

DATE/DAY	
PLACE I VISITED	
PEOPLE I MET	

DATE/DAY	
PLACE I VISITED	
PEOPLE I MET	

DATE/DAY	
PLACE I VISITED	
PEOPLE I MET	

DATE/DAY	
PLACE I VISITED	
PEOPLE I MET	

DATE/DAY	
PLACE I VISITED	
PEOPLE I MET	

DATE/DAY	
PLACE I VISITED	
PEOPLE I MET	

DATE/DAY	
PLACE I VISITED	
PEOPLE I MET	

DATE/DAY	
PLACE I VISITED	
PEOPLE I MET	

DATE/DAY	
PLACE I VISITED	
PEOPLE I MET	

DATE/DAY	
PLACE I VISITED	
PEOPLE I MET	

DATE/DAY	
PLACE I VISITED	
PEOPLE I MET	

DATE/DAY	
PLACE I VISITED	
PEOPLE I MET	

DATE/DAY	
PLACE I VISITED	
PEOPLE I MET	

DATE/DAY	
PLACE I VISITED	
PEOPLE I MET	

DATE/DAY	
PLACE I VISITED	
PEOPLE I MET	

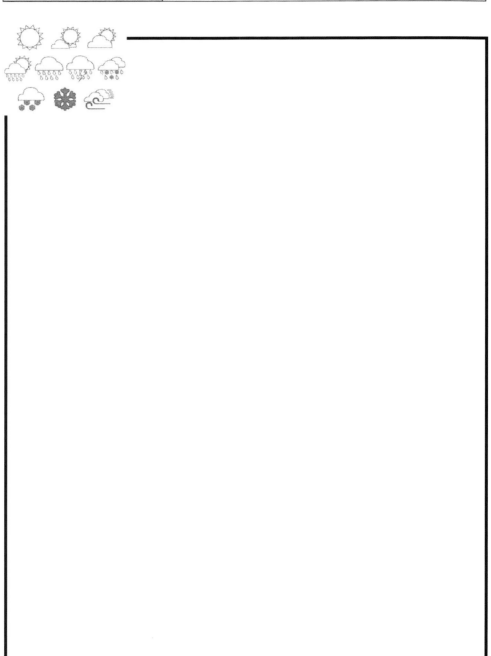

DATE/DAY	
PLACE I VISITED	
PEOPLE I MET	

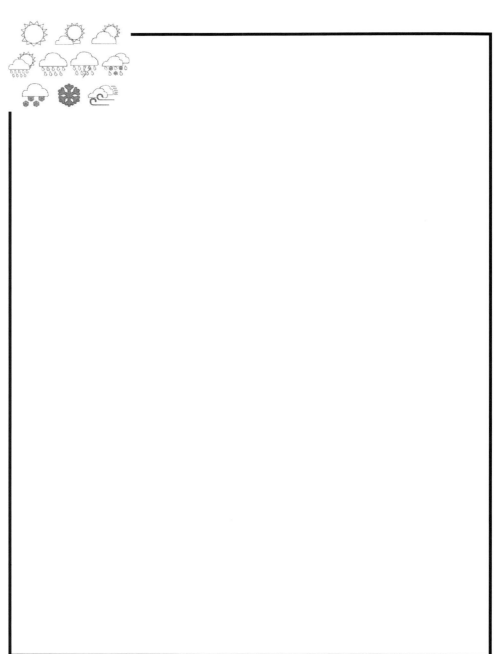

DATE/DAY	
PLACE I VISITED	
PEOPLE I MET	

DATE/DAY	
PLACE I VISITED	
PEOPLE I MET	

DATE/DAY	
PLACE I VISITED	
PEOPLE I MET	

DATE/DAY	
PLACE I VISITED	
PEOPLE I MET	

DATE/DAY	
PLACE I VISITED	
PEOPLE I MET	

DATE/DAY	
PLACE I VISITED	
PEOPLE I MET	

DATE/DAY	
PLACE I VISITED	
PEOPLE I MET	

DATE/DAY	
PLACE I VISITED	
PEOPLE I MET	

DATE/DAY	
PLACE I VISITED	
PEOPLE I MET	

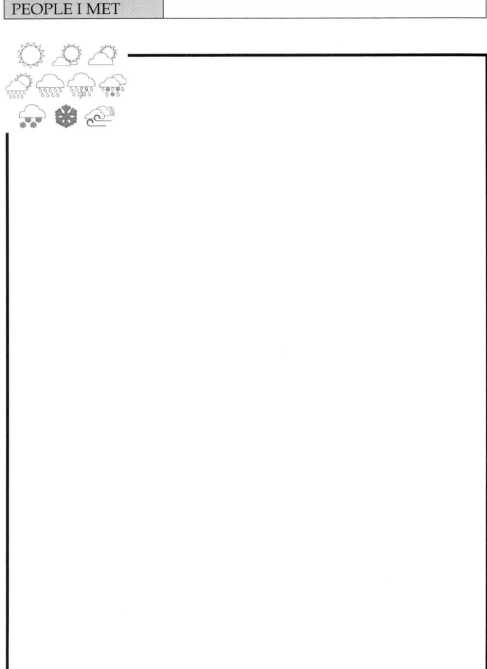

DATE/DAY	
PLACE I VISITED	
PEOPLE I MET	

DATE/DAY	
PLACE I VISITED	
PEOPLE I MET	

DATE/DAY	
PLACE I VISITED	
PEOPLE I MET	

DATE/DAY	
PLACE I VISITED	
PEOPLE I MET	

DATE/DAY	
PLACE I VISITED	
PEOPLE I MET	

DATE/DAY	
PLACE I VISITED	
PEOPLE I MET	

DATE/DAY	
PLACE I VISITED	
PEOPLE I MET	

DATE/DAY	
PLACE I VISITED	
PEOPLE I MET	

DATE/DAY	
PLACE I VISITED	
PEOPLE I MET	

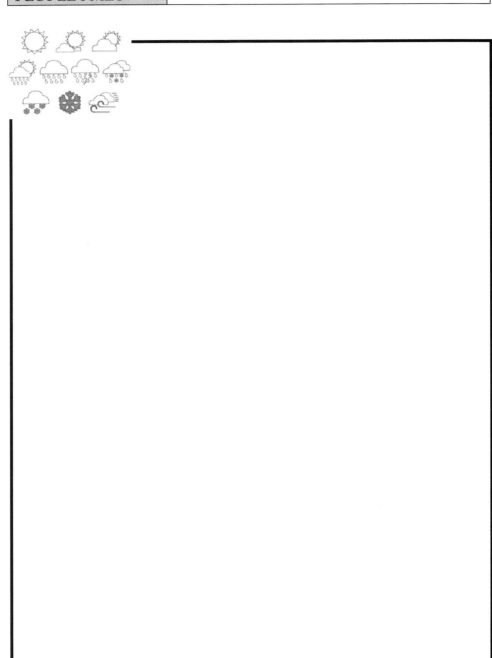

DATE/DAY	
PLACE I VISITED	
PEOPLE I MET	

DATE/DAY	
PLACE I VISITED	
PEOPLE I MET	

DATE/DAY	
PLACE I VISITED	
PEOPLE I MET	

DATE/DAY	
PLACE I VISITED	
PEOPLE I MET	

DATE/DAY	
PLACE I VISITED	
PEOPLE I MET	

DATE/DAY	
PLACE I VISITED	
PEOPLE I MET	

DATE/DAY	
PLACE I VISITED	
PEOPLE I MET	

Name	
Address	
Home	Work
Cell	Fax
Email	
Birthday	
Notes	

Name	
Address	
Home	Work
Cell	Fax
Email	
Birthday	
Notes	

Name	
Address	
Home	Work
Cell	Fax
Email	
Birthday	
Notes	

Name	
Address	
Home	Work
Cell	Fax
Email	
Birthday	
Notes	

Name	
Address	
Home	Work
Cell	Fax
Email	
Birthday	
Notes	

Name	
Address	
Home	Work
Cell	Fax
Email	
Birthday	
Notes	

Name	
Address	
Home	Work
Cell	Fax
Email	
Birthday	
Notes	

Name	
Address	
Home	Work
Cell	Fax
Email	
Birthday	
Notes	

Name	
Address	
Home	Work
Cell	Fax
Email	
Birthday	
Notes	

Name	
Address	
Home	Work
Cell	Fax
Email	
Birthday	
Notes	

Name	
Address	
Home	Work
Cell	Fax
Email	
Birthday	
Notes	

Name	
Address	
Home	Work
Cell	Fax
Email	
Birthday	
Notes	

Name
Address
Home	Work
Cell	Fax
Email
Birthday
Notes

Name
Address
Home	Work
Cell	Fax
Email
Birthday
Notes

Name
Address
Home	Work
Cell	Fax
Email
Birthday
Notes

Name	
Address	
Home	Work
Cell	Fax
Email	
Birthday	
Notes	

Name	
Address	
Home	Work
Cell	Fax
Email	
Birthday	
Notes	

Name	
Address	
Home	Work
Cell	Fax
Email	
Birthday	
Notes	

Name	
Address	
Home	Work
Cell	Fax
Email	
Birthday	
Notes	

Name	
Address	
Home	Work
Cell	Fax
Email	
Birthday	
Notes	

Name	
Address	
Home	Work
Cell	Fax
Email	
Birthday	
Notes	

Name	
Address	
Home	Work
Cell	Fax
Email	
Birthday	
Notes	

Name	
Address	
Home	Work
Cell	Fax
Email	
Birthday	
Notes	

Name	
Address	
Home	Work
Cell	Fax
Email	
Birthday	
Notes	

Name	
Address	
Home	Work
Cell	Fax
Email	
Birthday	
Notes	

Name	
Address	
Home	Work
Cell	Fax
Email	
Birthday	
Notes	

Name	
Address	
Home	Work
Cell	Fax
Email	
Birthday	
Notes	

Name	
Address	
Home	Work
Cell	Fax
Email	
Birthday	
Notes	

Name	
Address	
Home	Work
Cell	Fax
Email	
Birthday	
Notes	

Name	
Address	
Home	Work
Cell	Fax
Email	
Birthday	
Notes	

Food Available

Weather Experience

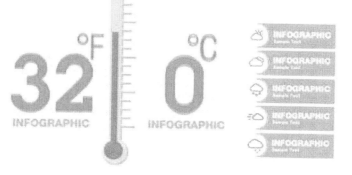

Manufactured by Amazon.ca
Bolton, ON

27098879R00061